POEMS FOR LISTENING

MUSIC FROM A BREAKING WAVE

DENHAM GRIERSON

COVENTRY
PRESS

Published in Australia by
Coventry Press
33 Scoresby Road
Bayswater VIC 3153

ISBN 9781922589033

Copyright © Denham Grierson 2021

All rights reserved. Other than for the purposes and subject to the conditions prescribed under the *Copyright Act*, no part of this publication may be reproduced, stored in a retrieval system, or transmitted in any form or by any means, electronic, mechanical, photocopying, recording or otherwise, without the prior permission of the publisher.

Catalogue-in-Publication entry is available from the National Library of Australia http://catalogue.nla.gov.au

Cover design by Ian James – www.jgd.com.au
Text design by Coventry Press
Typeset in Fontin

Printed in Australia

Contents

Foreword 7
Introduction 10
Acknowledgments 11

Prelude 13

Wave 14
Phone Call 14
Jazz at the Bowl 15
Joy 16
A Day 17
When 18
Two Years Old Grandson 19
Birthday 20
Chaos 21
In Between 22
Winning 23
Achievement 24
Meeting 25
Before and After 26
Bees 27
Revolt 28
New World 29
Change 30
Train Journey 31
Pea Soup 32
Skyscraper 33

Image	34
Wrist Watch	35
Machine	36
Twittering	37
Tourist	38
Constitutive of	39
Earth	40
Nest	41
Excellence	42
Weather	43
Balloon	44
Turning Over	45
Interlude	**47**
Grape Growing	48
Hermit Crab	49
Memory 1	50
Memory 2	51
Incense	52
You Cannot Know	53
Kicking Dust	54
Set Aside	56
Salmon Story	57
One Small Hand Speaks	58
Nostalgia	60
Just A Minute	62
Ascent	64
Imagine That	65
Wonder	66
Spaceless	68
To Do To Make To Be	69
Singularity	70

The 13th Hour	72
Messenger	74
Dystopia	75
Old Books	76
Pen	77
Sleepless	78
Conversation of the Living	79
Handle	80
Hare	81
Travelling	82
Stuff	83
Jazz Singer	83
Ochre Unfolding	84
Illusion	85
Conviction	86
Postlude	**87**
Lost World	88
Deafness	89
Welcome	90
Mistaken	92
Australian Summer	94
Lists	96
Longing	97
Where Will I Find You	98
Sawubona (I See You)	100
Speechless	102
Norse Legend	103
Encounter In Another Land	104
Proverb Explored	105
Preaching	106
Fixedness	106

Chess	107
Jingle Bells	108
Changing Clothes	108
Loss	109
Jessup and I	110
Paranoia	112
Tide	114
Say It Again	115
Commodification	116
Unity	117
Landscape	118
Orchestra	119
Lead Pencil	120
Balance	121
Nothing To See	122
Another Time, Another Place	124
Phoenix	126
About the author	127

**Previous books of Denham Grierson
published by Coventry Press**

Turning in Time
Sharing Water by the River

Foreword

Greetings to all you resilient ones who have the fortitude to delve into an introduction as well as the heart of this series of offerings from our friend, colleague, and fellow searcher for poetic vision, Denham Grierson. As in Denham's previous collection (*Sharing Water by the River*), the image of water is a significant focus in this collection of poetic exuberance.

> *Turning to tomorrow's rising ocean*
> *Sea music singing in my ears*   **Wave**

Found here is voice of one of our eminent forward-thinking, theo-practitioners who continues to be overwhelmed by the ocean of universal love and the on-going waves of profound change, together with experiences of knowing well beyond the rational.

> *Moving to a new place is a finding*
> *You cannot know until you get there*   **You Cannot Know**

Where the saying comes from I am uncertain but it is said that the presence of organised religion can be compared with being sold bottled water on the bank of a clear running river. A packaged semi-certainty in plain sight of the freely available wisdom of deep-life.

This is not you, Denham.

> *Learn to swim in ambiguity*
> *Buoyed by the tide*   **Tide**

What I find here in this delectable coming together of well formulated and expressive words is an invitation to be entranced by the mysterious wonder of everyday life for those who have the eyes to see!

> *Tasked to do, to make, to be*
> *To bring into being a unique life*   **To Do, To Make, To Be**

In this collection Denham opens up many dimensions of life to our minds and imaginations, releasing us to listening in ways that will always be uniquely our own.

> *Hold out your hand*
> *Rain falls between our fingers*
> *Grains from the hour-glass sand*
> *Will tell you that love lingers*   **Nothing To See**

With him and through him, we are immersed in everyday images combined with the unexpected pondering fostered by such pages of creative expression. We are invited further into the heartland of practical wonder, surprisingly, dangerously.

> *Falling wide and panoramic*
> *Carried by lazy waves*
> *Foaming as they break*
> *On golden beaches*   **Jazz Singer**

Thank you, Denham, for again plumbing the depths for us and being 'a finger pointing at the moon'. We treasure your unveiling to us a seeing of our mysterious underlay as human travellers; valuing the lucidity and lyricalness of your words, that call us to find in our here and now experience stunning new insights of meaning. Sure, often masked by the surface turmoil of the always in turmoil seas and oceans. But underlying the waves a confounding joy always there.

Let the waters flow!

John Cranmer

Introduction

In the Celtic world, authority lay pre-eminently with the King, then the Druids, followed by Poets. There was deep trust in poetry's vision. Poetry illumined and retold the past. Poetry orchestrated new images of the future, offering possibilities, calling forth intentionality. Poetry invited celebration and thanksgiving. Poetry spoke of what we cannot speak, that dimension we call the ineffable. Poetry disturbed the accepted order and gave rise to fresh thought. Poetry sought out the extra-ordinary buried in the ordinary.

The gift of poetry is that it offers newness, birthing metaphors and images that open to us unexplored ideas, un-named dimensions of experience, offering possible other selves, more sensitive, more complete. It is the voice of deep time we hear, flowing through daily events, that current that carries the mystery of things, the uncanniness at the heart of life.

When we share the meaning of our life we draw water from the ground source, the river of being in which we are immersed and from which we drink daily. Or to change the image, it is that music which comes to us on each breaking wave of daily experience out of the depths of an oceanic otherness that addresses us directly.

It is difficult to find a language that carries the meaning of this conversation. That is the unending task of poetry. To translate the music we hear as untranslatable and place it in our hands as a poem for meditation, enrichment and joy. An enterprise, however assessed, that carries its own authority, its own authentication, to our minds and hearts.

Acknowledgments

These acknowledgments read, or should read, like notes of a team meeting.

Again Mavis Grierson did the copy writing, Su Grierson the photograph, Hugh McGinlay the editing and presentation, Marelle Harisun and John Cranmer over-view and advice concerning poems chosen. John also wrote an Introduction. Always, the support of Nicci Douglas and Coventry Press.

Much could be said of each person's contribution to the whole but it has been said heartfully in previous publications. It seems here a needless repetition. But the sentiment remains the same. Thank you. We did it together. It is a genuine delight to be of one mind and intent with much loved people. No author could ask for more.

Prelude

Wave

Slowly the dark strip swells
Grows, rises, ascends, conquers
Rearing up, roaring on, foam fringed
So much depends on timing

Lifted up by countervailing currents
Into a heaving aqueous embrace
Smothered by a driving deluge
Momentum, propulsion, trajectory apace

Weightless, cascading exuberance
Speeding to the beach, denying caution
Cast up heavy legged upon resisting sand
Turning to tomorrow's rising ocean
Sea music singing in my ears

Phone Call

The regular phone call from the mine
To the home is to say
All is well, a safe exit today

Should the call not come
At the expected time, anxiety begins
Some disaster yet unknown

We are all waiting for a call
That reassures us all is well
Worryingly, time is stretching out

Jazz at the Bowl

Jazz at the Bowl, the monthly date
High anticipation of the quintet's play
The vocalist applauded much of late
We wait creation's celebrative way

New threads appear in patterns well rehearsed
The muse descends into the flowing stream
Birthing fresh ideas, children of the breaking forth
A tapestry novelle in all its themes

Each instrument performs, piano, saxophone
Bass, drum and voice
The unique solo, slipping back alone
Into the waiting scheme there to rejoice

The unrecognised familiar seeks us out
Declaring surprising variation
We are lifted by the novelty of chance
The gift of improvising notions

A human group, identity intact
Individuals well affirmed and sure
Subservient to the group as to a pack
Communal bonding into a seamless flow

The music calls to us at tumbling speed
To join this primal feast of sharing bliss
A powerful calling to our deepest need
Luxuriating in the cosmic Yes

Joy

Joy is not bliss
Not even happiness
It does not claim
A special name

Embedded in the flesh
Renewing afresh
The human touch
Our world as such

Abiding deep inside
Within this moment's tide
A gift beyond telling
Transcendence overwhelming

So it was this way
Upon a brown clad day
The weather soft and mild
Born to us, another child

A Day

A day of busying
A day of losing things

A day of holiday packing
A day of household checking

A day of quiet wondering
A day of magpie singing

A day in sunshine warming
A day of hanging washing

A day of small trajectories
A day of reading histories

A day of sorting mail
A day of test and trial

A day tireder, older, seeking bed
A day celebrating life as daylight fled

When

Excitement spreads of a new find
Dated before the Fifteenth Century, a Kilma coin
Perhaps from Tanzania, 1000 years ago
Found on the Wessel islands, near Arnhem Land

An early visitation on the coast
Portugese sailors, a coin survival
Who looted in 1505 the Kilma host
A minted coin 500 years before James Cook's arrival

Three hundred years before Dutch sailors
Telling of white tread upon Australian strand
Long before history books declared sojourners
A colonial presence on the island's sand

My Aboriginal friend is mightily perplexed
At the turmoil this coin has stirred
First Nation artefacts, 150,000 years old exist
Time of the Dreaming, have you not heard

Political speakers declare with pride
This is our country, no boat people here
These are our borders, our countryside
We have been here more than two hundred years

Two Years Old Grandson

You wouldn't would you
Yes, you would
I never really understood
Even when you wouldn't
And really shouldn't
Yes you would
Not because you couldn't
But because you could
Not considering shouldn't
Even when you should
Even when you said no
Yes you would
I don't intend to argue
That you should
Knowing full well
That if you shouldn't
Yes you would
Not because you misunderstood
But because I asked
You wouldn't would you
Of course you would

Birthday

The completed sweater
For all its brightness
Carried an air of quiet resignation

A heaviness that had pervaded
Its texture over the months of grief
Despair had flowed through the needles

Into the coloured woollen balls
As they knitted together
Giving the whole a pervading sadness

I like it, she said
Turning this way and that
Before the mirror

A slow smile creeping across
Her tired pinched features
Warmth covering her body with light joy

She glanced at me
A look I could not fathom
It is a beginning, she said

Chaos

The flap of a butterfly's wing can cause a hurricane six months after, half-way around the world.   Lorenz

Chaos rules the cosmos
And much else besides
According to predictable patterns
Which chaos derides

Chaotic systems have
A short term memory
Unreliable celestial knaves
Not to be trusted clemency

Oddity is the paradox
Order birthing chaos
Chaos being orthodox
Someone has a dice to toss

If you then seek order
To regulate the sky
Chaos will come suddenly
Transported by the wings of butterflies

In Between

In between the tightening arms of the vice
      agreed and seeking more advice
In between the lost and found
      the stirrup and the ground
In between the country and the city
      importunity and sitting pretty
In between a hard place and a rock
      the momentary tick and tock
In between the sour and the spice
      ugly crud and all things nice
In between hang about and time to go
      and saying yes and saying no
In between a quick surmise and longer look
      the shopping list and present book
In between the having and having not
      remembering and I forgot
In between what was and is to come
      and having all and having none
In between the quiet calm, the mounting panic
      the basement and the attic
In between the just begun and what is finished
      the always present, the newly vanished
In between the gamblers toss
      counting gains, enduring loss
In between to reap and then to sow
      what to doubt and what to know

      Life is always lived somewhere in between
      Assured purpose and all is not as it seems

Winning

The weight of our significance
Is feather-like within the scale of things
But not for those who love us
Whose judgment lies within the joy we bring

What endures is not a life's achievement
But what is held within the heart
Memory of the status of externals
In a family's life a distant part

What makes us who we are
Is human caring
A nurturing, a listening, a being there
Harvest of a deeply held believing

This is the treasure that never rusts
A reaching out, a reaching for, a reaching in
A fullness that we can truly trust
Faith, hope, and love, the formula of how we win

Achievement

A sense of reverence had eluded him
No feel for nature's beauty
Merely an economic smorgasbord
For growing enterprises surely

Disdainful of religious fervour
Dismissive of all sacred books
Committed to more acquisitions
Accumulation, and how things look

Bewildered by the idea of the holy
Unimpressed by any sacrament
He insisted on demonstrable achievement
Which, if God exists, is what God really meant

Full of advice to overcome our ignorance
Wisdom wrapped in every cliché's saw
Like my business, you need a snappy slogan
A hollow one, stuffed to the gills with straw

Meeting

When I told Jessup
Loneliness was a recognised disease
He was astonished

He flung his hands to the sky
Moved them North, South, East, and West
What then of these my friends

The sun, the wind, the rain
Each with its own accent
In daily conversation

Morning bird calls
Night meeting with evening stars
Embracing warmth of the earth, our mother

He looked at me with incredulous eyes
How is it possible to be lonely
When all of life is meeting

Before and After

Because of his mother's mental illness, the poet Lawrence Ferlinghetti was placed in an orphanage for a time before being adopted by his aunt. Later, unexpectedly, his mother and brothers arrived at his aunt's home, where, aged 6, on the front lawn, he was asked to choose between the families. He finally stuttered 'Stay here'; his whole life decided in an instant.

Before and after have a doomsday content
Gravely a formal message sent
A sense of matters getting out of hand
The tumbling of time's grains of sand

In the first case, anticipation of the highest kind
In the second, doubt, will the decision stand
Knowing there is no return to before after
Promised outcome of tears or laughter

As if the future is balanced on a pin
All resting on a roulette spin
This instant seeking a guiding voice
Destiny's outcome in the choice

Do we then hold life in our own hand
Feet seeking balance on a slender strand
An act that carries no less than all
Rising into joy, perhaps a fateful fall

This is the agony of finite sight
Seeking what is wrong and what is right
Believing in the freedom of our will
At the end we wonder still

There is no passage to the waiting shore
If choice does not breach the wall before
No knowledge comes until after
Acted certainties do not alter

From many options we chose one
Believe it good when it is done
Nothing lost now it is so
All at stake solved long ago

The pen writes on the page
Mark of a fool, sign of a sage
At last, for good or ill, our name
We are expected just the same

Bees

The bees from Jessup's hive
Had left on mission
Purple growth on the North slopes
Attracting their attention
Time for cropping, time for harvesting

I spread honey on bread and butter
It is not often, Jessup said
Life puts itself utterly
Into your hands. I was not sure
Whether he was referring to bees or honey

Revolt

Civil unrest happens
When feelings of powerlessness
Reach critical mass

Critical mass comes to expression
Leading to tidal violence
When voices are not heard

Inevitably the blunt instrument
Of coercive power is employed
To crush the people's opposition

Driving resentment and anger
Underground where seeds of
Rebellion and anarchy are planted

All that is needed is to listen
Brute power is deaf
The merry-go-round goes round again

New World

There is a new recipe
For constructing society

Control language
Legitimate lies
Distort reality
Sow confusion
Suppress dissent
Subvert the law

Willing consent is needed
Controlled by arrogance

Naiveté
Complacency
Commercial greed
Wishful thinking
Fearful compliance
Indifferent apathy

Making our culture great
Eliminating freedom

Change

We do not welcome change
Resisting its offer
Denying its summons
Unwilling to concede the game is over

Defending the house Capitalism has built
Myopically repeating failed strategies
Rhetorically justifying that which is dire
When clearly the building is on fire

I suggested climate change
Requires radical new thinking
Readjusting economics and ethics
To a changing reality

He rose from his chair, walking away in anger
As if there is another place to go
Denying what everywhere is obvious
The house is on fire even so

One inescapable force
We cannot avoid try as we will
Change remaining the one constant thing
That daily knocks upon the window sill

We can resist, eschew, deny
Apportion blame, redouble ire
Against implacable reality's reply
Do you not see, the castle is on fire

Train Journey

Rolling across the desert plains
The train develops a soporific chant
Inside calm and detachment
Soft seats, air conditioning
Resolutely the tracks define
Direction and terminus

Outside bounding mobs, long necks running
Dust clouds from brumby galloping
Across vanilla slice stretches
Below Florentine rock clusters
With spinach bushes on the rise
Spinifex sharp pointing
To an endless blue stretching sky

Double glazing keeps the sounds away
Willy-willy dust denied space
No experience of raw desert
Invades the leather seats of first class
Ensuring passengers travel uninstructed
About wildness and bleached bones
That tell of generations at one with desert life

Pea Soup

Under which cup does the pea reside
Is it real or an illusion
Constantly moving from side to side
Seemingly without intent or reason

Is the world I see the world that is
Substantial, unassailably real
No mysteries behind its surface
It is what it is, with accessible appeal

The pea moves to another explanation
The world I see is shaped by me
Perception paints each new creation
I participate in earth, sky, and sea

A third cup waits to raise a question
The world does not exist apart from me
Without my willed, imaginative description
There is no world at all, no moving pea

The conjurer makes visible and invisible
That which we seek to gain
Suggesting by a choice we name the probable
As likely as a thesis to explain

So we struggle to possess reality
To reassure that what we know is so
Pea soup tales of human culpability
Tantalising cups of yes and no

Skyscraper

Thin, pencil skyscraper
472 metres tall, $100,000 a square metre
$95 million for the Penthouse
Among the clouds, rich, superior, distant
Height without weight, outlook without insight

Never to trip over a neighbour's dog
See ducks dabbling in sparkling water
On the village pond
Or find a crocus flower in a rock crevice
To feel rain upon the face, nevertheless

There are two worlds here displayed
Haves who, elevator sped, rise upwards
Have-nots, who, bewildered, gaze skywards
Newsprint wrapping wind around their feet
Wondering if the height has news of God

Neighbourhood clatter, cries of children, traffic noise
This is the sound of what we are
In the luxurious pad, heaven's address
Is manufactured silence
Less and less human as we glide higher, higher

Image

His image is spread ubiquitously
Throughout the city
Star burst across a vast commercial sky
Turn a corner there he greets you
Car drivers on the freeway meet his smile

When he sees his own wind-furled image
Festooning streets and roads and lanes
Is there identification with this person
Or indifference to a stranger self unknown
Created by a hard worked advertising drone

Making promises that cannot be kept
Offering assured integrity
Based upon a well honed sporting skill
Satisfaction if they buy what he is selling
Thin as his paper image on the bill

If there is depth where to be found
Here the ephemeral dressed up to make appeal
For a time an offer never to be repeated
Is there in this image something real
He smiles, the wrapping on my fish and chips

Wrist Watch

My wrist watch is a litmus test
Not of time passing, or moral decline
But of a failure to greet the sun
Since its life force is solar defined

When through exhaustion it lags
It still tells me the time
I have too long spent reading new books
In old leather chairs supine

Failing to stride forth heroically each day
Allowing light to charge its tempus predilection
I have shuttered its task by lethargy
A reckless disregard for action

Here is a device that speaks of light
Which is the hidden source of time
Warning of the coming of the dark
In its robotic way drawing a line sublime

Machine

Upon the plains of nature
We construct virtual realities
Clever and complex
Confounding the simple and innocent

Compulsive on this path to maximise
The artificial
Arms length from organic life
Harsh critic of untidiness

Convinced the economic tide
Will lift the raft of daily desire
Ignoring the distant roar of rapids
Disintegration of community

Google will light my way
Cook meals, wash clothes
Heat rooms, play tunes
For me, entirely alone

A machine world without heart
Un-acquainted with ambiguity
Clearing a space for new invention
Enemy of life's intention

Twittering

Only sparrows and wrens twittered once
Now a whole generation does
Believing it is the way things are, must be
Email, search, tweet and texting endless scree
Tapping blindfold between the real and virtual

A matrix of interlocking sign and symbol
Sustained by scrolls, clicks, moods, and repetition
Trolling a civic duty, comprising self-hood
Electronic act entrapping, thought to be understood
Fragile as a flicked switch, decreeing darkness

Where is the centre in this scouring flood
Of nothing much, religiously pursued
Within this endless stream of natter spewed
Ephemeral chattering worlds
Where spirit has no reason to be named

Tourist

The siren call is to become a tourist
To trip lightly over complex issues
To be lavishly fed, indulged, distracted
Returning with a video of distant wonders

On the magical, romantic journey
One will not engage the hidden slum
Or people on the edge of starving
Poor, neglected, lost, time rendered dumb

There will be anecdotes, travel stories, small disasters
To fill out the narrative of the journey's challenge
Without disturbing the complacency of travellers
Who do not question their entitlement or carriage

You would not believe they sold boiled rats
In a market where rubbish filled the lanes
Or children even, it was said, in whispered voices
Some people have it hard, I felt sorry for their pain

Constitutive of

The earthworm is useful but not beautiful
The tiger beautiful but of little use
Necessary in creation's schema
Each dependent on the other

The deep has no sight yet is profound
Height is not wise but does have sight
Which is the way to find direction
Each but a mirror of the other

Backwards carries memory's weight
Holding options few
Forward has a world to give
Hopes of far and true

There are those who travel fast
Others only travel slow
The one makes gains but does not gather
The other takes time to know

Water, liquid in the hand
Running on to pastures new
Rock motionless across the land
Foundation of the river flow

The dung beetle is useful but not beautiful
The peacock is beautiful but of no use
But those who choose the one above the other
Are short-sighted and obtuse

Earth

You
can
see
from
here
the
view
is
clear
above
mountain
trees
and
streams
All
is
not
as
it
seems
The
air
is
a
pretend
This
is
where
it
ends

Nest

We arose to the news
That the black swan
Had abandoned her nest
Where she had sat for days

On the morrow it was occupied
By ducks aware that safety
Was now offered them
As they taught their young with pride

Is there a nest waiting for us
A sanctuary of safety
Where we can rest protected
Giving birth to new vitality

Excellence

Not that way, Pa
He took the brush from me
Impatiently
Sought more paint
Returned to the canvas
Reflectively
Added here and there
More colour sought
Intuitively
Spread with intention
In a swirl of composition
Creatively
Leaning back satisfied
There! One so young to hold
A vision of excellence

Weather

Weather reports predict heavy rain showers
Interspersed with passages of sun
Stretching throughout the week

We waited expectantly, dismayed
As days passed bearing little
Or no resemblance to predictions

Storms visited adjoining suburbs
Where vegetation stood up, watered and grateful
While empty clouds scurried past us, drop-less

There is now little trust in us
Concerning tomorrow's predicted sunny day
We have gum boots, coats and umbrellas ready

Balloon

He was unto himself a burning bush
From which he spoke *ex cathedra*
Brooking no dispute, pronouncing absolutes

He was to himself a pointing finger
Point and counter point all righteousness
Defining directions, demanding obedience

He was to himself an infallible compass
Spelling out destinations, unvaryingly assured
Constantly on true North by definition

He was unto himself a weather vane
Revealing which way wind and currents ran
Shaping, guiding and defining the world

He was unto himself an emperor
With requisite dignity and roman nose
A ruler unaware he had no clothes

He was unto us a red balloon
Susceptible to a pin prick by a child
Held aloft by hot air and decayed illusion

Turning Over

How do we know it is over
When it is over
How do we know it is done
When it is done
How do we discern
The final wager
How understand the turn
From skip ahead to lagging ager

How recognise the quiet dismissal
Accepting that the race is run
Stepping aside without denial
Celebrating our time in the sun
Not seeking to hold the disappearing
Nor pretending that the time has not yet come
Out of the chrysalis a new appearing
Let then go to greet what has begun

Interlude

Grape Growing

Teeth clenched vineyards stretch
In severely disciplined rows
Into regimented distances
Long years of ordered service

Some have early leaves
Budding under pale sun
Other plantings show no signs
Strung along wires, at attention

Same weather, same environment
Mystifying difference between plots
Different varieties growing disparately
Organic variance displayed

Growth, pace, persistence
Is not predictable
If one seeks calendar precision
In its own time fullness will come

Teaching has this limitation
However planted, watered, stimulated
Fullness comes in its own time
Mysterious as the ripening grape

Hermit Crab

Surrounded, by dangers swept
Seeking a shell fortress
To prevail against all threat
Safe in a home's protection

Growing bigger, reaching out
Painful recognition shows
That which masquerades as safe
A threat to that which grows

Vulnerable again
Into the ocean hurled
Leaving what is home
To seek a larger world

Terrified, defenceless, all at sea
How can one expand
When all that's reassuring
Is lost upon the sand

In order to find peace
A house with greater room
Reaction to the threat
Destiny, the child of doom

Memory 1

Forgetting is freeing
Sometimes it leaves us lost
Remembering a feasting
Sometimes not

Memory's thread binds up the wound
The story teller carries
Distant baying of the hounds
Warns we cannot tarry

Bread crumbs on the forest floor
Travelling on an unknown way
Coming back to where we were
Memory fading of each day

Photos on the window sill
Pain and joy a duet song
Soothing notes and echoes shrill
Searching out where we belong

We are conjoint memories
Much wiser, also sadder
Are we the sum of stories
Climbing Jacob's ladder

Memory 2

Memory has its assignment
To hold artefacts, museum's store
Gathering objects of purpose
Testimony to living lore

Memory has responsibility
To give direction along the track
Charting a way, looking forward
By wisdom learned many lives back

Memory kindles the fire
To warm us in seasons of cold
Smoke-drift of consciousness
Stories of loved ones of old

Memory knits us together
You, me, and others as well
Gives to our self-definition
Confirmation of life's magic spell

Incense

Sandalwood smoke shadowless
Slow ascendency, invisible substance
A mirage of being, gossamer sprite

Bearing in its latency shrouded obscurity
Tendril cast skyward in abstraction
Twirling, twisting on unseen currents

Birthing in its insubstantiality
A fragrance of untold, unseen things
Perfume in a fog of imagining

Lifting the spirit to follow its tracing
Out of its nothingness a drifting promise
That powerlessness will bring us home

Holding us to that which will endure
Even as its cloudiness disappears
A staircase carrying us to hallowed enchantment

You Cannot Know

You cannot know until you get there
Messenger to Mercury over many years
Your five year old self to eighty five
You cannot know until you get there

What you know will be transformed
Wisdom takes a lifetime to grow
Beckoning through many changes
You cannot know until you get there

Each step unveils new insights
To be put aside as contexts change
A fresh stage summons with its promise
You cannot know until you get there

Be patient in your journeying
There is much to learn along the way
Moving to a new place is a finding
You cannot know until you get there

Kicking Dust

Kicking dust, a well developed skill
Of those destined for Capital Hill

Involving mind and heart and will
Conjured up within the rumour mill

Proverbial in the saying 'dry as'
Capable of creating chaos

Masquerading, obscuring vision
Substance of Mandrake illusion

Valued in political melees
Blinding purpose in affrays

Around the Cabinet table they say
To keep the circling pack at bay

Not just aided by drought
Conspicuous when fire's about

Dedicated to make it hard to see
The difference of to be and not to be

Shared with chosen newspaper articles
Display of the quantum particle

Which might in fact be seen as wave
A promising career to save

Dedicated to control the restless mass

Interlude

When written down just balderdash

They come wanting to believe
Dust cloud they receive

More powerful than wanton lust
Without substance, only husk

Carrying a soothing thrust
Who else can you trust

Set Aside

We are set aside, now we are old
Removed, symbolically speaking, to the back shed
Companion of the bakelite wireless
The jagged toothed crosscut saw
Burnt out appliances, the Beta Max
Pinned butterflies on calico
Dried flowers between pages of
Hard backed tomes confined to dusty trunks

There is no harshness in this gentle unobtrusive slide
An air of quiet concern, almost parental
We cannot properly operate a mobile phone
It is better then we, once comfortable, be not consulted
No longer guardians, protectors of the realm
Much loved totems in brown and purple
Who offer reassurance not quite certain
And measured calm if needed

There is a blindness here, an unawareness
More a lack of insight than exercise of will
We are deeply alive, creatively hidden in our stillness
Beyond the lure of limitless horizons
Living in a liberated listening zone
Wrapped in a restful wisdom
Of a certain mode and style
They too will come to know

*Salmon Story**

The salmon came to teach
The people how to pray
This is the first story

The second story breaks open
Laughter, which entertained
The gathered people for hours

The third story brought the people
To their feet dancing, reconnecting
To the earth with stamping feet

I wish such a salmon
Swam in the deep waters
Of my consciousness

Teaching me to pray
To laugh, to dance
With a trinity of stories

From a sacred story of the Spokane River people.

One Small Hand Speaks

Hebrew is a language of the Image
Greek of parallel lines and distances
There is a home to be found within the one
Thickets and gorse abound within the other

One calls forth the fragrance of sage, rosemary and thyme
The other leads into the complexities of space and time
There are the psalms, the dance, the song
The other wrestles with what is right and what is wrong

One offers wisdom in the form of parable
The other a god-struggle, pounding on the table
The first committed to the coin specific
The second birthing glory and the epic

My native tongue is neither, language of the Bard
To penetrate into the others is dispiritingly hard
If pulling on my boots to make a pilgrimage
A Guidebook in each language would be leverage

For each language without fail
Defines the end of road and trail
If each could be followed to the end
I doubt that we would share a final bend

How then a shared language of love
A common perspective of below and of above
I hold the tiny fingers of my son's son
A time when speech has only just begun

Interlude

Flesh of my flesh, bone of my bone
In varied worship we all differently intone
Let the very earth cry out, stone by marbled stone
Not to love each other is what we must atone

Each small hand leads us back to our own birth
Before the separation cry that leads to earth
Here is our home before the tribe, the village and the heath
Before the distance of the words we learn to speak

Nostalgia

All of life hangs on the thin thread of conversation.   Ernst Becker

Two men converse across a camp fire
Beside a tranquil lake
Light from the flames illuminating their faces
A pale moon dazzles the lake surface
Pine trees lean in to listen
Their tent behind gathers small breezes
In the falling gloom

A time when Environment in situ
Invited conversation
With the natural World
Pine smell impregnated air
Quiet forest glade whispers
The gathering of wholeness
The kinship of created things
That arouses even now nostalgia deep within

On the train to town
Conversation has fallen into disuse
Eyes fixedly exploring flashing screens
Filling and emptying images
That carry nothing important or permanent
Or are evocative of Nature's allure
Manufacturing realities
Constructing electronic dwelling places

One cannot detect here
Sharp wood smoke's caress
No pine fragrance redeems the hungry air
Only a muffled cough, a scuff of shoe
A sense of alienated space
Where to dwell? Where to rest
Tapping his screen, answering a call
Disembodied reality in a virtual train

I close my eyes remembering
When life was filled with vital otherness
The warm glow of evening coals
Night birds calling, bush rustle
Intimations of a gathering storm
Flapping the tent wall even now
Deep affirmation of human sharing

Along the platform, heads down
Passengers move with purpose
Still spell-bound by their phones
Surrounded by metallic voices
Loudly declaring scheduled times
A chill wind sweeps the emptiness
No true warmth without, within
I wonder who is dying in the silence

Just A Minute

Just a minute of your time
Is not a feckless ask
It has to do with mindfulness
As you contemplate your task

You do your work with thoughtlessness
A measure of indifference
Does the cock at morning crow
Know what we reap and what we sow

I contemplate the words that bind
Redemption of the silent kind
Between the stirrup and the ground
Mercy sought and mercy found

Eternity in a grain of sand
Or is it in a drop of water
No easy answer comes to hand
The flash of axe, the unexpected slaughter

There is in this moment much to say
It has a weight we may yet garner
To lose the meaning of the day
Disregard its hidden wonder

So good then to talk in this small moment
No big matter in the scale of things
But as you sweep up after consider
All the treasure that it brings

Interlude

The clock rings out from the bell tower
Ponder our time together, brief, congruent
The register of sweet and sour
No big deal, it was just a minute

So much in these few seconds
Closing his eyes the Doctor shakes his head
We grasp a little of his meaning
It takes but a minute to be dead

Ascent

You are never finished, Jessup said
Every gain threatens a loss
Wisdom's store is assaulted by temptation
There is decay in all things we possess

Not much fun, you might conclude
Each day a new beginning
Susceptible to slipping wasted away
The true gain is in renewing

We enter into creation
In every act to bring new light
Overcoming the darkness of destruction
How else to rise above the earth in flight

So saying, he set the pigeon free
Where it lay, caught in a trap
We watched it lift above the sea
Rising above death's loosening grip

Imagine That

In mathematical physics there is an imaginary number i
The square root minus one a magic power
Unlikely cosmic key since non-existent
Revolutionising algebra, befriending geometry
And by its entry into consciousness
Phantom force constructing quantum theory

Bringing authority to domesticate time
Confounding abstract, nebulous, drifting ether
That defines three fold space dimensions and more
Directing into our rational grasp
A formulaic highway carrying us
Into a city of realistic solidarity

The imaginary I is not unknown to us
Searching out a way to unify our world
Conquering myriad uncertainties
That assault our growing selfhood
Reassuring us on our stumbling path
We all live in constructed realities that are imaginary

*Wonder**

This warm porridge habitat
In which we live
Is miraculous

Our seasons are the gift of
The tilt of earth's axis
Hospitality's inclination

The moon, accompanying au pair
Feeds us with tides
That carry life

Jupiter's guardian galaxy
Filters cascading space debris
To shield us from assault

Earth's molten core
Protects us from the sun's
Destroying rays

Plants and trees together
Give us the oxygen
We breathe to live

The list of benign forces
Enabling this nurturing world
Is beyond computing

A delicate balance within a narrow band
That makes our species viable

For our short span

Inside this nest
Our very being shares

*With acknowledgment to James Phelan
'E.T. won't be calling' in a letter to
The Guardian Weekly 31 August 2018.

Spaceless

No start, no end
No entering or exiting again

No boundaries, no still point in a turning world
No climbing mountains, or martinis whirled

No end of night, new day begun
Exercise at the gym, the morning run

No move towards, moving away
No wandering, no sheep astray

No sunburn, droughts, or flooding rains
No pond or bush or tree or endless plains

No against, knock, search, or ask
No rising early to address the daily task

No height to reach, no depth to plumb
No measuring by glance with outstretched thumb

No coming wave, no fleeing light
No need to spray the apple blight

No sense of warm, no sense of cold
Of being young and growing old

Existence does not stamp its foot
No fires to light, no chimney soot

Time has helped me clearly see
Without space there is no place to be

To Do To Make To Be

We are a constituting consciousness
Putting together a world of meaning
I do not intend just to do something
I seek to be someone

This intention is a stretching towards
To have a mind, a purpose, a design
So significant as to carry destiny
Into the choices made each day

We are not just moving towards
There is an anticipated destination
A deep down desire to take care of
We tend to our self, to others hopes

This active forming of a world
Requires imaginative participation
A running conversation of wish and will
To comprehend, to plant, to nurture, to grow

The only way to reveal myself to myself
Is so to act at building a lived in world
In which we can be safely together
To sing, to dance, to be joyful, to be still

Tasked to do, to make, to be
To bring into being a unique life
Moving through its measured time
Celebrating to the full the gift of birth

Singularity

Poetry is a pious pretence
Artefact of childish innocence

The poet, captivated by Utopia
We look down twin barrels of dystopia

Memories of childhood retreat
At the bottom of the garden war and deceit

Flutterings of words in literary nests
Flying away from viruses and pests

Blanketing our world with words
Ignoring flying arrows, glinting swords

A Morris dance of tinkling bells
Unmoved by facts disasters tell

Turning from the crushed of earth
To weigh a word and judge its worth

What use are flowery fantasies
Among the din of feuding dynasties

Hunger, drought, financial press
Crafting a line of measured stress

Addiction to sweet nursery rhymes
No coinage in the sphere of crime

Where else the cosmic yea
Against despairing nay

Erasing 'serves you right'
'There's hell to pay'

Without poetic innocence where spirituality
Awe and wonder spring from singularity

The 13th Hour*

Has the thirteenth hour struck?
Tin drum beating out a hollow sound
'Fake news is true', 'A word means what
I want it to'. The lie is truth's corrective

Has the clock struck thirteen?
A fife marching with the drum
Distorting truth, twisting speech
Serving a versionland of bigotry and grief

Is this the last time?
A present mirror of dystopia
Image on t.v. cruel, arrogant, denying
Shaping reality to its fell lying

Has time run out?
Attack of the past upon the future
Defending iron borders, racism's wall
Designed to intimidate us one and all

Has time run over?
Truth, liberty and hope
Are no longer in a living state
Alternative facts upon the slate

Has the clock struck an alarm?
Awakening us from sleep
Calling for a birthing of new deeds
No bed of lies grows tomorrow's seed

Interlude

Is this the clock's last call?
Tramp upon the street a marching band
Not yet marching feet. A knock upon the door
Precursor to a tale told once before

Has the doomsday hour struck?
A mounting chorus, self justifying
An anthem feeding growing violence
Where do we turn for solace

Does the clock herald a new day?
Resetting the hands of cruel fate
Overthrowing a distorted paradigm
Justice, faith and love rise up in time

*Reflection on 1984 in an Orwellian Age

Messenger

The sunlight on the snake's skin
Focused its intricate beauty
Carrying with it a hint of menace
Even so, I thought

Jessup looked at it dispassionately
A creature cursed by mythological weight
Of human fear and anxiety
In all its innocence

The true mysticism
Is to see things as they are
Ambiguously uniting beauty and threat
The natural order of things

Here is at once the symbol of evil
The light-bringer, who is God's servant
An exquisite evolutionary gift
Harmlessly asleep in the sun

He looked at me sharply
We do well to walk by quietly
That is how we give homage
Rendering me silently unsure

Dystopia

Hero systems of our culture broken
Trust has fled, we feel forsaken

Politicians wrapped in lies, we now despise
Walking election streets with sly deceit

Sporting stars in drinking bars
Coarsely spoken, often wanton

Musicians hired, drug dose inspired
Lyrics obscene in rapper dreams

Police obstruct, sadly corrupt
Dismantling order, crossing borders

Clergy urging silence, fermenting violence
Distorting spirit by commercial ambit

Super heroes substitute with special powers
Fantasy escape as daily living sours

Entertainment of the bomb and gun
Leaving no place to run

Culture-fashion prisons
Landscape without vision

Old Books

Hail comfort of much loved books
Each one a friend
Somehow still significant
From beginning to the end

Holding not only ideas
Recording steps along the way
Growth's slow progression
Even now, with something left to say

Names I spoke with reverence
Teachers that offered food each day
Calm and quiet and mannerly
Not often was I led astray

Light shining off assorted spines
Inviting reflection's play
No longer household sages
Still gold in each assay

Pen

It is audacious
To throw out of the cupboard
That which is old
In preference for the new
And foolhardy

Old and new belong together
Lean on the need to touch
Both then and now
For balance

I am not convinced
Shininess and gigabytes
Generate thought
I write this poem
With a pen

Sleepless

Large red numerals of the clock face
Are luminous in the darkened room
Sleep, elusive again, gone ferreting
I watch the numbers tumbling over

We have an allotted span, time to be alive
Not always industrious, productive
Infertile in this present sleeplessness
It would be wrong to feel obliged

Time is not our enemy, but an indulgent friend
Making us aware, chiding us, reminding us
Without time nothing would be at stake
Here is a concern that makes us mend

The numbers roll over in the silence
Curiously we are in communion
Nothing demanded, no exhortation,
Wry chuckle, checking up on me again

Conversation of the Living

I am not afraid of dying
The struggle is getting to the end

Perhaps God is an underachiever
She chuckles

I have no strength for a visit just now
Tomorrow the palliative people
Contact me to arrange the next step

I will ring tomorrow and each day
In case you have the strength
Graciously, that would be wonderful

Putting down the phone I wonder
When I call tomorrow

Whether she will have packed her bags
And gone to that place she calls home

Handle

It would be good
If everything had a handle
Most of the time
I cannot retain them

Great ventures slip
From my fingers
Intended tender acts
Escape beyond grasping

There are parts of life
I cannot hold down
And many possibilities
Oily as eels disappear

To grasp things securely
To hold them to our breast
Would be a real comfort
But they have no handles

Hare

The hare running across the path
Leaps the high jump wall into sanctuary
Frozen mid flight, light illumined
Brown white fur glistening, eyes bulging
Legs taut with effort intensifying lift-off

In this moment on infinity's edge
More than a hunted body pursued
Musculature stretched beyond visibility
Life surge lifts the hare's sensibility
Above rock, creek and earth

Telling time, camera click
Projectile intentionality held motionless
Escaping by means of aroused blood and fibre
Propelled by life, energy, and fear
Where does life go when it leaves

Travelling

Losing and finding
A life-time task

Seeking and binding
Is to be blest

Knocking, the opening
Received bequest

Holding and enfolding
To be home at rest

Being called quietly
Begins the quest

Stuff

Squeezing the empty tube
Declares the finitude of stuff
There never is enough

Jazz Singer

The burgundy tones
Of the jazz singer
Cast us into
Precipitous depths
Falling wide and panoramic
Carried by lazy waves
Foaming as they break
On golden beaches

There are messages here
Lost in translation
Compelling us to crack open
Chinese crackers of
The known, re-conceived
To read a promise
That in the catch of sound
We fervently hope
Will be fulfilled

Ochre Unfolding

Blue pottery bowl deep red dirt filled
Gathered from the edge of this wide land
Carrying the essence of the vastness
Fractured crevices of mountain fastness
Timbral dust of desert places

Here is the touch of arcane mysteries
Ochre markings, tribal signatures bestowed
Beyond recounting, reaching back to darkness
Deep time of the Rainbow Serpent passing
Lava pourings in the frost baked snows

Story telling origins of memories
Claiming of untouched tribal lands
Carried by the life beat deeply throbbing
Holding to a story surely coming
Of the red dust sand

Embraced by a fire cast coloured bowl
Witness of tribal sagas spawning
Thunder and lightning over endless Country
Named by ancestral spirits, flowing springs
Of the very stuff of time it sings

Witness of which we cannot tell
Iron seams within the arteries of life
Beside a pile of photographs, companions lost
They no longer grace this time, this place
A grass cross-bridge beyond our present space

A handful of red dust, witness to time's haze
Transparent present, Ancient of days

Illusion

All is illusion the great religions say
A magician's pass
Impenetrable impasse
A rock strewn way

All is ephemeral, great teachers say
Obscuring mist
A dancing twist
Deceiving, beguiling, a shadow play

All is to hand, they heard him say
Consider lilies in the croft
Wind clouds moving aloft
Life, marvellous and fey

All is in hand, he was to say
Rhythm and rhyme
In God's good time
Enfolding every day

Conviction

It was an impression only
Barely the blink of an eye
Perhaps a breath passing
A flicker across the surface
Of vision, gone in an instant

Banished from the corner
Of peripheral sight instantaneously
Yet consciousness registered
Its momentary appearance
Holding a vivid image

Immediately gone but real
So real it stayed as if
Stamped upon the retina
Having a reality not to be
Questioned, beyond doubt

Tho' it had no provenance
As evidence it had been
The image is efficacious yet
Phantom parallel to
Faith's deep conviction

Concerning the substance
Of things not seen

Postlude

Lost World

When my island disappears
Under the sea of global warming
How then will I know myself
Child of a particular cultural becoming

If a bout of homesickness
Sweeps over me in a strange land
To what will it refer
My homeland swallowed by the ocean

Taking with it, ancestors, family
Icons, sacred burial sites, and childhood wonders
How then will I know myself
Abandoned, lost, homeless forever

Deafness

There is a way of solitude
That must be negotiated
Having about it an abandonment
A sense of being cast out

There is a way of silence
To be travelled
With no warning voice
Or the whispering of herd wisdom

There is a way of darkness
That lays hidden snares
Unseen obstacles, waiting traps
Devoid of guiding light

But the fatal way is mundaneness
A greyness of un-attending ordinariness
That sucks life from the soul
Destroying the capacity for faithfulness

Here nothing sought, nothing expected
All without risk or elevating purpose
Absent a warning awareness
You are asleep, deaf to the music of eternity

Welcome

I am certain that Jesus
Did not fit easily into religion
That solemn cloak of shackled sobriety
Out of touch with hunger's laughter

He was too open to the wind
The earth's joyous song
Carrying the rhythm of present mercy
Within its flowing mystery

Too close to God's intimacy
A sense of presence in each breath
An endless delight in life's rapture
Celebration of living within grace

We battle on the surface
Erect tents of propriety, rituals, rules
Warding structures of institutions
Rarely free enough to welcome risk

With his open heart of hospitality
Inclusive embrace of those in need
Shepherd of the lost and straying
He kept no lists of people's shame

Politics and religion won in the end
Imprisoning him in fictions of respectability
Punishing him for breaking holy rules
For loving God above propriety

Postlude

That is where I meet him. On the road
Wind at his back, telling stories
Of a hidden Kingdom that warm my heart
If the door is locked, the key is under the mat

Mistaken

There is no doubt, the voices say, you are mistaken
The nature of experience does not support your claim
That which aspires to be an otherworldly omen
Is but the manufacture of your creative brain

There is no hidden ground, no secret source of being
Or spirit working to stem the tide of fate
We exist as one-off scraps of life's projection
The falseness of your doctrine clear both soon and late

You have made up the Presence that surrounds you
A spin to keep uncertainty and doubt at bay
Proofs of the transcendent are unconvincing
Stratagems and falsehoods to cover up dismay

No rational being can accept this fanciful concoction
No scientific mind support the manufactured lies
The only truth is one that can by experiment be tested
There is no other world beyond the sky

Fantasy is the staple of your believing scene
Piety the concealer of the unjust shadow
Zealous fictions fill the spaces in between
Of no account yesterday, today, tomorrow

God is a word as empty as a chime
The claim of a chosen figure, crucified and risen
A well documented waste of time
One wanders in a trackless desert seeking a decision

Postlude

The soul, a product of deceitful, cunning crafting
Identity, a phantom to cover up a hole
There is no power working at transforming
The whole charade exacts a tragic toll

So the voices chatter daily in my head
Seeking to persuade and to dissolve
Leaving me with questions I cannot answer
But conscious of an unnamed squirming unresolved

This nihilistic chant which claims to be true
Leaves us with nothing at the core
It is a wasted litany, erroneous each day anew
Faith does not need such pleading to be sure

Australian Summer

A blowfly at the feast
Like beer without yeast

A snake in the back garden
Like an approaching warden

A cockie in the sink
Like an elephant on the rink

A dead rat in the sewer
Like a politician's oeuvre

Wasps among the clover
Another picnic over

Mozzies in the living room
Presage of the crack of doom

Grasshoppers en masse
A reality t.v. rash

Ants in wild confusion
Like a bloody revolution

Breeding rabbits running riot
Like a nose bleed at the Hyatt

Midgies in descending cloud
Yet another soccer crowd

Shrieking seagulls at the beach
A squirming worm within the peach

Postlude

Fleas within the bedroom sheets
Losing at the noon day meet

Spiders in the overalls
Like panic when the Holden stalls

Red back on the dunny seat
Returning reveller's mid-night screech

Summer the Australian way
Like manure in the dray

Beyond all this an experience indescribable
The Tax Office says you're liable

Lists

If you want to avoid mortality
Draw up a list
Structuring time into busyness
To be seriously addressed or wished

Drawing up a list is virtue enough
Intentionality, sober and intelligent
Reducing life to a realistic frame
Solid, predictable, assured intent

Standing as a sign of ethical responsibility
This careful list of set tasks, desirable ends
Has the benefit of being endlessly repeatable
Even if, in the event a pretend

You will do more than get by with such a guide
Carrying that most desirable of all conceits
A means to conquer boredom, inactivity, and shame
The cloak we throw over the scythe leaning on the seats

Longing

The distant wail of a sea bird on a lonely beach
Will, without cause, evoke unnamed nostalgia
A drift of perfume on a passing riff of air
A smell of cigar smoke in a room of dusty chairs
A long glance into a dense dark forest stealth
Will call forth a longing that takes away the breath

In this reoccurring dream, a home well remembered
Warmth throughout, polished wood rendered
The smell of bread baking, off somewhere children's voices
Creaking stairs up to a bedroom, my name upon the door
I am sure, by force of logic, I have never visited before
I hear remembered Circus music, and above a cavalcade of stars

This longing is not easily discounted, no matter how hard I try
Entwined in all of memories traces, a background feathering hard to deny
Evoking a hunger that neither food nor flesh nor fame can take away
A cry from far astray, a call that has a reoccurring theme
More than the Piper at the crack of dawn, the silent promise of today
It gathers up all that matters and all that will come to play

So it is there, an unresolved inquiry, a persist wondering
Insisting that beyond all else, in this world strangering
Without the grounds for justifying this outlandish claim
The intense longing tells of a lost home we cannot name
Where we will carry all we truly love and cherish
And find waiting, beyond all hope, that which cannot perish

Where Will I Find You

Will I find you in the joyous leap
Soccer's forward somersault
Diving into unfathomable spirit
To its primal source
Drinking from this deep well
Of feeling

Will I find you questing in Plato's cave
Sorting arcane knowledge for a clue
Leading to upward climbing steps
To enlightenment beyond reason
Treasuring the gift
Of understanding

Will I find you reaching out
To wretchedness
Food for hunger, water for thirst
Seeing you naked and oppressed
Supplying love's desperate need
Of action

Will I find you in aching absence
Returning echo only emptiness
We have created, vacuum without
Oxygen to call forth a life
Of hope

Postlude

Will I find you in stillness
Asking, seeking, knocking
Waiting for your touch
Whisper that transforms the world
Promising endearment
Of rose petals

Or in this work worn dying flesh
Forsaken on rejection's edge
Powerless in a starless sky
Casting a word wreath
We call forgiveness

Sawubona (I See You)

The ancient wisdom says, Attend!
Look carefully at what lies before you
Enter into its open invitation
Only after reverent waiting, proper stillness

There is no certainty here
No promised gift, assured reward
For that would be a death. Distraction
Stay calm, disciplined, persistently aware

As an artist looks upon a rose
A scholar tracks the fading text
The mother touches her sleeping child
So one must look intently just to see

There is a boundless mystery even so
That what I see is the birthing of begin
Beneath a living Presence's golden glow
Beyond my wondering, my searching, and my ken

When you turn the key, unlatch the door
Lift the blinds, open the shutters wide
Speak softly of the matter of your heart
The magic garden of the soul within

I can but grasp the edge of you
That I that tests the boundaries of my eye
For what I see and what I hope to hold
I perceive because I have been told

Postlude

It is the gift of light by which I see
The hidden universe of inner space
Beyond imagining, beyond time and beyond place
The source of where, when, why, and how

A giving that answers the wanting need
bringing to shoot and branch and flower
All that sees between the you and me
The moving of the wings, the white Dove's power

Speechless

There is a language we have used, loved, cast aside
Holding us to commitments no longer binding
We look about for other words to speak, recite
But in the house they must be hiding

New narratives, new stories struggle to be born
The plot escapes us, dramatically unsure
We try a note, just now bassoon forlorn
Waves break up soundlessly upon a barren shore

Yesterday's assurances hushed, awaiting a new voice
Trailing into silence, seeking primal force
Casting off old habits, a compelling choice
Rendering us quite speechless, dumbfounded and perverse

Where are the fields to harvest
The buzz of vital conversation
Where is the Wind, the Spirit's onset, vesting
That would awaken words of consolation

Norse Legend

Yggdrasil, the World tree, in Norse mythology
Had three roots
The first, tended by women
Controlled the destiny of all things
The second, in the land of giants
Held secrets of the universe
The third, in the regions of the dead
Kept knowledge and magic safe

The World tree is dying
Women are denied their appointed task
Giants have died out, taking secrets
Of the universe forever
The realm of knowledge captive to propaganda
None of them of interest in a commercial age
Captivated by digital extravaganza

Over the earth spreads a poisonous mist
Choking and polluting Yggdrasil
Whose evergreen leaves drop dew
To renew and restore sky, earth, and sea
There is no remedy among the blind
Whose inhabitants cannot see
The sources of the world are drying up
We are losing what truly frees

Encounter In Another Land

The face of the old lady
Was fractured by tiny webs
Time had etched its story
Across its beaten surface gently

She rose to take my order
Her crutches clattering
Detecting my reaction she smiled
Old age is not for the fainthearted

Returning from the gloom behind her
She placed my order and a small box
In my hand, matches I had not ordered
You are a light bringer, she said

Light fires in the heart of your people
Without warmth and light
Life has no efficacy
Her blind eyes carrying a vision
I had never seen

Proverb Explored

Only a spoon knows a pot's sorrows
Only a spoon lifts pain beneath
Many spoons stay in the shadows
Passive, inert, a spurious peace

Cast and moulded to perform a task
Conceived to help in any circumstance
Unmoved by need or set intent
Unused, uncalled, by incident or chance

There is here a mystery stark
So much to offer, so much to give
Ready, prepared, designed for work
Not knowing how to live

Never tested, never proved
Safe within the cutlery cave
Waiting contribution never offered
Abandoned in a shallow grave

Preaching

Preaching is archaic, its capital long spent
A digital world finds it bemusing
Irrelevant to gaining daily rent
An exercise worth banishing

Labouring for words exegetically adept
Carrying stones up hills that roll down again
Holding quick-silver truth within a net
Cast in the sea surging within

How can one be dismissive
A stillness grows, a listening throng
Hearing in a plain discursive
A story leading to dancing and to song

Fixedness

Jesus was not a talker
Who spelled things out
More a caring doer
Moving about

Now fixed in stained glass
Dumb in a chattering world
Healing frozen fast
Banners now furled

Chess

Each day we play chess
With God. Our choice, moving a piece
Extinguishing countless options

Our aim to capture the Queen
Eliminating obstacles
To ravish her realm
Capturing her domain

God gathers up rejected cast-offs
Knights and Bishops
Restores ruined castles
Gathers defeated, suffering pawns

We, in our lust for conquest
Do not quite read the game
We seek to found our Kingdom
God, a Kingdom for the lost and lame

Jingle Bells

At the bottom of the liturgy sheet
It said 'Merry Christmas and
Jingle bells'
A slow creep of poisonous weed
Across the garden of
Good News
Disregarding the coming execution
Or the cost of being whole
Among disregarding revellers

Changing Clothes

Death is bearing down
Knocking at the door
Swinging the wrecking ball
Among my friends and peers

There is no point in protest
We do not hold the cards
Discernment leaves no options
They're digging a grave yard

A place of final terminus
For bones and blood and flesh
Time to put off old clothes
To try something fresh

Loss

Weather rolls over us, changing expectations
Beyond our power to overthrow
Conscious of planning under threat
This moment, this hour, tomorrow
Who is to know

Balls spin in casino halls
Chance balanced by inviolate laws
Mis-step, uncertain stroke, wrong choice
All is at hazard in this pause
Who is to know

Change and chance define our daily toil
All ventures provisional and unsure
Caught within a vice of dual force
There are no tactical escaping doors
Who is to know

Be present, Merciful One, in our travail
We, who are wearied by change and chance
That we may rest in that which is assured
Unafraid of what might fall
As those who do not know

Jessup and I

We talk together, Jessup and I
He has no sense of disembodied spirit, he claims
In touch rather with green spring shoots
Water pond dragonflies, composting ant-hills
And the coming Apocalypse if
Bee populations are destroyed by herbicides

He seems always to have his fingers
Deep in rich loam, cutting fresh kale
For me, warning of grasshopper hordes
Telling me to fix the roof before flooding rains
Arguing that agriculture must be recovered
From economic spread-sheets fertilised by greed

When I talk of God's purpose he is impatient
His fork throwing up weeds more vigorously
I have no time for useless reflection
That does nothing to bring the earth
Back to life from our reckless slaughter
His faded blue eyes glaring at me

We walk across bumpy paddocks
Relieved of last season's crop, resting
He seems to be in silent communion
With the rhythm of their life patterns
Pointing to cawing corella flocks
Speeding away on invisible wind gusts

Lunch under canvas by the old farm house

Postlude

Bread, cheese, and home-brewed beer
His sun damaged hands embracing a glass
He, somehow as rooted in the soil
As the ghost gum above us leaning
Into one of our conversations of eternal things

Paranoia

If you are suspicious
Nothing is as it seems
Underneath the surface
Malice flows in ordered streams

If you are suspicious
Nothing occurs by chance
Behind the accidental
An orchestrated dance

If you are suspicious
Everything is connected
Random events are really
Phantom images projected

Governed by dark design
All is working clandestine
Forces active and malign
Never to be trusted any time

Paranoia sees the world as fake
Soil already poisoned
Shadow cast upon the stranger
Hatred bred without apparent reason

If you are suspicious
They are wrong and you are right
Doubting the motives of the other
In a universe of black and white

Postlude

If the corner stone is trust
A willingness to believe the best
Without love reaching for another
Truly there is no place to rest

Tide

The rip corkscrews away
Arrowing to deeper water
Capturing the unwary
The unattending

Go with its urgency
Seek its edge
Be carried into deep water
Escape into fathomless possibility

Learn to swim in ambiguity
Buoyed by the tide
That you cannot control
But carries you to your destiny

The illusion of freedom
Will remain intact
Unseen currents
Will do their work

Out into the open place
Seized by the unknown
There before your awareness
Waiting for your coming

Say It Again

I have said it once
I will say it again
Without hope
Where can you begin

I have said it before
Below, above
The death of personal
Means death of love

I have said it often
Almost beyond belief
If there is no trust
How can there be faith

I will say it once more
Ignorance is no excuse
Faith, hope and love
Are your essential truth

Commodification

With great success Capitalism commodified Divinity
Buddha statues in the garden, Shinto shrine at the gate
Rainbow snake, a camper van enhancement, an oddity
Tree of life, a tattoo on the skin, precisely shaped

Menorah on the BBQ, angel image soars
Christ child, embossed cherubic face
Yin and Yan on the flapping bar room doors
Crescent moon hanging above the drinking place

Hallelujah chorus selling a money lending bank
Celtic holy jewellery, totem images, carved wooden scrolls
Banner selling Lent as a flavour event
Icons in multiple variety, a scarf's sacred whorls

Here are wondrous symbols, post-modernity rolled flat
To pin upon our walls or decorate our gardens
No longer carrying intimations of the numinous
An outwardness from shops that offer countless bargains

No access available, there is no depth
Meaning banished without context, not understood
Except as artefact on fashion's plinth
Blindness displayed, assassin of our inwardness

Unity

It has been said
Spirit is the unity
Of power and meaning

Power without meaning
Is blind, brute force
With no explanation

Meaning without power
Is a peculiar helplessness
That suffers endless torments

Spirit for its part
Needs embodiment
To be truly effective

Body without spirit
A lost creation
Waiting redemption

All of this bound together
In the courage to be
Nevertheless

Landscape

Black wattle corpses litter the slope
Above the wetland vastness
Their limbs separated, now habitat
For small animals and copper-heads

Cackling merrily, biker fires
Sweep up the slope, destroying all refuge
Poisonous smoke from blaring exhausts
Sending tremors across terrified flat lands

Leaving behind blackened graffiti
On the decimated slopes, mourning
The loss of self and memory
Of days of bee song and blossom fragrance

There is a story here, told endlessly
A returning myth of renewal
Worm Uroboros, the endless cycle
Of the seasons, life, death, rebirth

It is not enough to bring reassurance
Nor a satisfying explanation
The source of life evades our grasp
Alongside teeming wet-land ponds

Orchestra

The orchestra which is my life
Is tuning up as I wake
Becoming conscious of the quiet practice
Hidden preparation, industrious beginnings

There are discordant notes sounding
Clusters of strings, wind instruments, tympani
Fitting into co-ordinated tribalism
Gathering together of one accord

Harmony begins to assert itself
Calling for a unified tapestry
Of intricate and far reaching sound
Focused by baton consciousness

I hope today the music of my life
Going forth to unknown listeners
Will carry themes and narratives
Full of joy, gladness and celebration

The score resonating with creation's song
A hallelujah chorus of delight
At being one with all that is
Life's cadenza giving praise

Lead Pencil

(Meditation in a palliative care ward.)

The sharpener shaves away
Protective layers
Bringing to functionality
A sharp operating point

Ready, the HB2 moves to its task
Spelling out humanness
Fragility the cost of usefulness
Pressure snaps the moving press

Blunt, defeated, the sharpener returns
Cutting away defensive, constraining wood
Restoring essence brutalised
Sharpening vocation once again

Upon the white page
Of unmarked possibility
Imaginings writ large
Treaties, love poems, scribble's exuberance

Reducing, vanishing in productive action
Unused stub now resting idle, put aside
Miraculously whole, mission complete
Efficacy not lost in disappearance

No alchemist transmutes the pencil lead
To burnished gold
Time's eraser eliminating all trace
Of daily commerce and a story told

Gripped in a guiding hand
Sharpened again to be
Eternal mark now possible
Fulfilment pencilled in

Balance

Equilibrium must recover from stretching
Intense compaction and lack of attention
In order to maintain balance we can trust
Golden mean, middle way, wire of suspension

Springing back to readiness against irrational forces
Anxious to advocate the edge, the bet, the test
Paying little attention to the follow through
What must be protected from fatal risk

The future cannot be set always
At hazard, without protecting with care
Countless myriads of organisms
That share our earth, victims of gun and snare

We must tread upon this soil with reverence
Aware of what can precipitate our fall
Seeking to balance opposing forces
Protecting the one, the many, the all

Nothing To See

There is nothing to see
The tube is hollow
The noise you hear
Is yesterday's bellow

There is nothing to wait for
Time has passed by
We argued on the shore
Blood pressure rising high

There is no point in making plans
They shall not reach fruition
Toil of our minds and hands
Will end only in confusion

There is nothing in the vault
That can save the day
It is nobody fault
We are being swept away

There is nothing to redeem
The failure of our race
Nothing so it seems
Puts us firmly in our place

Why then the froth and bubble
Pretence at miracles now done
It is just toil and trouble
That should never have begun

Postlude

If only we had patience
To walk humbly without pride
Too much stubborn resistance
To take the given in our stride

There is nothing to be gained
By grasping after more
It is an old refrain
It has all happened once before

Look if you will
On every side
To seek an answer still
The arrow will fly wide

Hold out your hand
Rain falls between our fingers
Grains from the hourglass sand
Will tell you that love lingers

Another Time, Another Place

Lunch at an old friend's place
Was to enter another world
Of cobbled lanes and narrow streets
That, like spider threads, lived off
The broad limbs of public roads

Twisting and turning among worker cottages
Along bypaths obscure and secret
Where muffled instructions, covert orders
Were given to messengers with hooded lanterns
Following agendas of the night

I listened for the clop of covered hooves
Looked for horse droppings at ancient corners
A proud belonging in complex networks
Of a neighbourhood of sealed lips
And little understood tribal loyalties

Suddenly one is cast into a square
Council uplifted with architectural polishing
A shiny plaque declaring beside a water fountain
'Dedicated in 1867 for community use'
Under the gaze of two-storeyed gentrified dwellings

Bluestone fences topped by iron grills
Leading along tessellated paths to high gloss doors
Testifying to garages filled with Volvos and Land Rovers
Passing by the hidden life of worker cottages
Unaware, certainly not comprehending this invisible host

Postlude

Here quiet people live who drink at the community fountain
Renovating their timber dwellings with care
Chiselling old values into restoration with fierce zealotry
Keeping picket fences white and memory of another time
Young couples, refugees from upwardly mobile squares

Moving away from abandoned gaslights on tall iron poles
I plunge back into the labyrinth of streets and lanes
Arriving at last, hearing the distant noise of modern traffic
That has little efficacy where I sit stamped, 'Visitor
Duration Three Hours'. Stranger in a strange land

Phoenix

There is no escape
As far as we can tell
From black cloaked death
Resolute, implacable
Ashes to ashes
Dust to dust
Crematorium's climactic

But dust and ashes
Are your native heath
Fleeing life beyond its killing stroke
In order to emerge again
From hell's fiery realm
Complete and whole

Legendary one of wondrous creation
You have your nesting deep within
Carrying us to our destined ending
Calling us into life again
Lifted by the Spirit's vivifying power
The promise of the Christ to give

Spread then your magnificent wings
Over the benediction of our lives
Out of fire let your song sing
Praising life that never dies
Carrying us to where we shall be home
Great feathered servant of the sovereign God

About the author

Denham Grierson, Uniting Church Minister and retired academic, agrees with the claim that poetry is the music of time. Not just now time but universal time, an enterprise that seeks to hold the elusiveness of our inner experience, the attempt to grasp sunlight that for a moment illumines the mystery of our being. Poets also read books, play golf, listen to music, garden spasmodically. But always with an ear to the music of time and its timeless magic.

www.ingramcontent.com/pod-product-compliance
Lightning Source LLC
Chambersburg PA
CBHW011317080526
44588CB00020B/2741